D1501778

What People Wore
During the
American Revolution

Allison Stark Draper

The Rosen Publishing Group's
PowerKids Press™
New York

For my mother

Published in 2001 by The Rosen Publishing Group, Inc.
29 East 21st Street, New York, NY 10010

Copyright © 2001 by The Rosen Publishing Group, Inc.

First Edition

Book Design: Emily Muschinske

Photo Credits: p. 3 © SuperStock; p. 4 © The Granger Collection; pp. 5, 6, 7, 9, 21 © Civil War Foundation; pp. 8, 10, 11 (all photographs), 15 © Jeffrey Foxx; pp. 11, 14 (illustations) © Emily Muschinske; pp. 12, 13 (shoe) © Archive Photos; p. 13 © CORBIS; pp.16, 17 © North Wind Pictures; p.18 (prickly pear cactus) © Derek Hall/Frank Lane Picture Agency/CORBIS; p. 18 (grinding) © Alison Wright/CORBIS; p. 19 © Hulton-Deutsch Collection/CORBIS; p.20 © Sophie B. Steel courtesy of *Historic Dress in America*; p. 22 © Rich T. Nowitz/CORBIS.

Draper, Allison Stark.
    What people wore during the American Revolution / Allison Stark Draper.
      p. cm.— (Clothing, costumes, and uniforms throughout American history)
    Includes index.
    Summary: This book describes what people wore in the days of the American Revolution, discussing the uniforms of both American and British soldiers, the simple clothes of the Americans, and the fabrics that were first manufactured in America.
    ISBN 0-8239-5666-0
    1. Costume—United States—History—18th century—Juvenile literature. 2. United States—History—Revolution, 1775-1783—Juvenile literature. 3. United States—Social life and customs—1775-1783—Juvenile literature. [1. Costume—History—18th century. 2. United States—History—Revolution, 1775-1783. 3. United States—Social life and customs—1775-1783.] I. Title. II. Series.

GT607 .D68 2000
391'.00973—dc21   00-039163

Manufactured in the United States of America

Contents

Settling and Trading

Beginning in the early 1600s, British settlers came to America. These men and women settled in **colonies**. Most still felt very connected to England, however. They dressed in the same style of clothes that they had worn in England. They also

traded with England. The colonists sent tobacco, oil, and furs to England. England sent shoes, boots, stockings, and blankets to America. In time, the colonists began to feel more American than British. They were tired of paying money to the British government, but not having a say in how the colonies were run. The Americans also paid much more for British clothing than people in England did. This made them angry. The Americans wanted their **independence** from England. The British did not want the Americans to be free. This led to the American Revolution, a war that started in 1775.

Before the American Revolution, England and the colonies traded goods with each other.

Colonists dressed the same way that they had in England. This man is wearing a long coat called a frock coat, a waistcoat, or vest, and a ruffled shirt.

Made in America

In the years right before the Revolution, Americans tried to wear clothes that were made in America, not England. Once the war started, England blocked America's ports. The Americans could not get goods from other countries. They had to depend on homemade clothes. There had not been much **manufacturing** in America up until then. Fabrics in America were not as well made as fabrics from England. Thomas Jefferson, who later became the third president of the United States, thought that most American fabric was uncomfortable and ugly. He thought that Americans would go back to buying goods from England after the war.

Once the war started, Americans had to make their own goods. Even young girls were taught how to sew.

Most Americans believed in their need to be independent from England. The men in this picture are wearing frock coats and waistcoats. Some are wearing triangle-shaped hats called tricornes.

Brown to Begin

At the start of the American Revolution, it was decided that the American army would wear brown uniforms. This decision was made by George Washington, the head of the American army, and other leaders. The British army wore red uniforms. There were many different **regiments** in the American army. Each had different **facings** on their uniform. Many men did not get their uniforms, though. It was hard to find cloth. Soldiers ended up wearing whatever color uniform was available. They also wore **tricorne** hats, black belts, and boots. They carried long knives called bayonets that attached to the end of their rifles.

At the start of the war, soldiers wore brown uniforms. ➤

This young soldier is wearing a tricorne hat with a place for him to carry a spoon. Supplies were hard to find, so soldiers made sure to hold on to whatever they had.

Simple Clothes for Hard Work

Working men who were not at war dressed in simple **breeches**. Over the breeches, they wore leather vests, jackets, or aprons. Some craftsmen wore waistcoats, a type of vest. Men on the **frontier** wore **buckskin** breeches. Men also wore linen hunting shirts or jackets that had **fringes** on them. The fringes let water drip off. Women wore clothes that let them move freely when they worked. The first layer of clothing was a linen nightdress called a shift. Over that, women wore ankle-length skirts. The upper part of their outfit was called a **bodice**. Women wore aprons to protect their clothes. They wore soft cotton or linen caps called mobcaps.

 Men and women dressed in plain, comfortable clothes that made it easy for them to work.

A woman's first layer of clothing was a shift.

This canteen is made from a turtle shell. A canteen holds liquid and is made of metal or other material.

Women's dresses did not have pockets built into them. Instead women tied pockets around their waists with string.

Colonial men wore breeches that came down to their knees. They also wore waistcoats with loose-fitting shirts underneath.

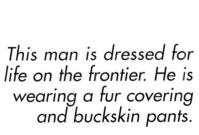

This man is dressed for life on the frontier. He is wearing a fur covering and buckskin pants.

Dressing in the Best

During the American Revolution, wealthy women still dressed in fine fabrics. However, some wore less fancy styles. Abigail Adams, who was married to future president John Adams, dressed in **conservative** clothes. She wore a black bonnet, a short **cloak**, and high-heeled shoes. Abigail Adams thought it was important that women dressed in clothes that made them look neat. One popular piece of clothing was a wrapover dress. This dress was

This man and woman are at a ball. She is wearing a dress with a square neckline and a jacket with a looped-up hem. The man has on a frock coat made of fine fabric, breeches, and shoes with buckles instead of laces.

made of **muslin**. This dress was worn with a jacket over it. If the jacket had a straight hem, it was called a caraco. If the hem was looped-up, it was called a polonaise.

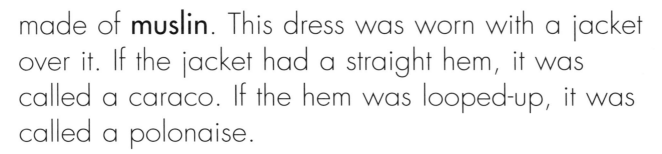

This woman is wearing a dress with a square neckline, which was popular during the time of the Revolution. Wealthy women could afford to have lace and other fancy trim on their clothes.

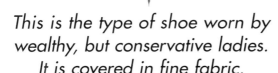

This is the type of shoe worn by wealthy, but conservative ladies. It is covered in fine fabric.

Fine Gentlemen

By the late 1700s, men's coats were shorter and narrower. Waistcoats also got shorter. They were usually made of the same material as the coat. Coats were cut away in front, so more of a man's breeches could be seen. The breeches became more fitted. Breeches ended just below the knee and were worn over stockings. They did not have zippers. Instead breeches had a square flap that buttoned up. Men's shoes were made from cowhide or buckskin. There was no difference between the right and left shoe. Both shoes were the same. Most shoes had buckles instead of laces. For fancy events, men wore shoes with small heels and thin soles. These shoes were called pumps. Pumps looked like ladies' shoes.

Instead of zippers, men's breeches had square flaps that buttoned in front.

14

Men wore short, powdered wigs. Some had ponytails that they wrapped with pieces of dyed cotton.

In the late 1700s, men began wearing shorter waistcoats.

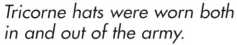

Tricorne hats were worn both in and out of the army.

When they dressed up, wealthy men wore ruffles on their collar.

The Powder Room

Fewer men wore wigs in the late 1700s. Those that did wore short wigs that had curls on the sides. The best wigs were made of human hair. Others were made of yak, goat, or horse hair. Wigs were powdered with perfumed flour. Men who wore wigs shaved their heads. They wore caps over their bald heads at night.

Men and women also had their own hair oiled and powdered. They protected their clothes by covering

 By the late 1700s, men were wearing shorter wigs. The wigs were powdered with perfumed flour.

them with a powdering jacket. They protected their faces by hiding them in a paper cone while a servant sprayed powder over their heads. The servants sprayed the wealthy man or woman with nearly a pound (.45 kg) of flour! The richest people had a special room for this purpose called the powder room.

This is a picture of a wig store. The best wigs were made out of human hair. Others used yak, goat, or horse hair.

Beetles and Beauty Patches

Many women, and even some men, wore makeup in the late 1700s. At the time, it was in style to have a very white face. Flour and cornstarch were used as a makeup base. Red rouge was used to highlight a woman's cheekbones. Rouge and lip color were made from an insect called a cochineal beetle. This cost a lot of money, so poorer women used berry juice instead. Eyelashes and eyebrows were kept neat with fine-tooth combs. Beauty patches were small, black patches that were put on the

Red coloring is made from the type of insect on this cactus. The British army used this dye, or coloring, to make their uniforms red.

The man shown here is crushing the insects used for red dye into a powder.

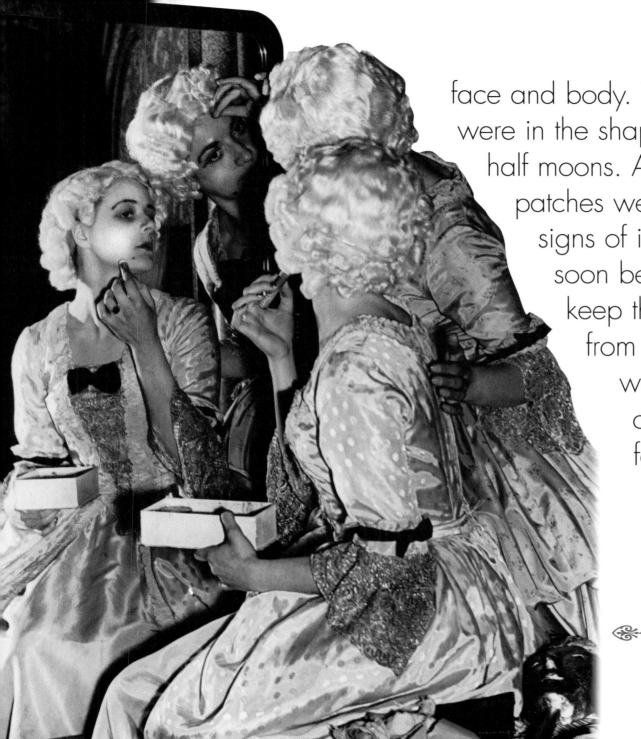

face and body. These patches were in the shape of stars and half moons. At first beauty patches were used to cover signs of illness, but they soon became stylish. To keep their skin safe from the sun, wealthy women sometimes covered their faces with masks.

 It was in style for women and men to have very white faces. They got this look by using flour and cornstarch as a makeup base.

19

Following Their Parents

Both boys and girls wore linen dresses until they were five or six. A child's dress had a full skirt and a tight bodice. The bodice had strings attached to the back. The strings were used to hold on to a child while he or she was learning to walk. Some small children wore puddings. A pudding looked like an inner tube and was put around a child's middle. This way a child would not get hurt if he or she fell down.

When children turned five or six, they began dressing

The young children in this photo are wearing simple, muslin gowns. Children dressed like this until they were five or six.

These children are dressed like adults. The boy has on a frock coat and breeches. The girls are wearing simple dresses. The girl on the left has on a mobcap. The girl on the right is wearing a coat called a cloak. She keeps her hands warm by keeping them in a tube-shaped piece of fabric called a muff.

20

like their parents. Wealthy girls wore silk dresses with **corsets**. Wealthy boys wore fine waistcoats, breeches, and silk stockings. Some young men even wore wigs. Children did not just dress like adults. They were expected to act like adults, too.

Blue at the End

Toward the end of the war, the American uniform changed to blue coats with red facings, and buckskin breeches. Cloth for uniforms was ordered from France, an American **ally**. Many soldiers did not get their new uniforms, though. These soldiers had to mend the uniforms they did have, which were often nearly rags. They had to wash and fix the coats, then put them together again. Even without proper uniforms, the soldiers won the war against the British in 1783. In 1789, George Washington became the first president of the United States. He took his **oath** in a dark suit made out of American cloth. Washington was proud of his country and of the goods, including clothing, made in America.

This man is dressed like General George Washington. He has on the blue uniform worn by American soldiers at the end of the war.

Glossary

ally (AL-ly) A group of people that agree to help another group of people.

bodice (BAH-dis) The upper part of a certain type of woman's dress.

breeches (BREE-chez) Short pants that cover the hips and thighs.

buckskin (BUK-skin) A strong, soft leather made from the skins of deer.

cloak (KLOHK) A heavy, blanketlike cloth worn around the shoulders.

colonies (KAH-luh-neez) Areas in a new country where large groups of people move who are still ruled by the leaders and laws of their old country.

conservative (kun-SER-vuh-tiv) Following traditional styles.

corsets (KOR-sitz) Undergarments worn around the middle of the body that are tightened with laces.

facings (FAY-sings) The collar, cuffs, and trim of a uniform coat.

fringes (FRINJ-ez) Trim made of threads or cords, either loose or tied together.

frontier (frun-TEER) The edge of a settled country, where the wilderness begins.

independence (in-dih-PEN-dents) Freedom from the control, support, or help of other people.

manufacturing (man-yoo-FAK-cher-ing) The business of making something by hand or with a machine.

muslin (MUZ-lin) A cotton fabric.

oath (OHTH) A promise to follow through on what you say you will do.

regiments (REH-jih-mentz) Groups in the military.

traded (TRAYD-ed) To have bought and sold goods.

tricorne (TRY-korn) A hat with three corners turned up.

Index

Web Sites

To find out more about what people wore during the American Revolution, check out these Web sites:
http://www.walika.com/sr/uniforms/uniforms.htm
http://www.colonialwilliamsburg.org/life/clothing/home.html